˝The Only Cook Book˝
on
The Hidden Secrets of Buckwheat

"More Than a Cook Book"

Inspiring ancient methods, naturally gluten free. Wholesome, age
proven (grains and seeds) compilation (recipes).

Helping you learn how to cook and bake with naturally gluten free buckwheat,
milled flax seeds, milled chia seeds, and oat bran.

Dedicated to those who are on a gluten free and diabetic diet.
Recipes using coconut sugar for those who are diabetic,
and cane sugar for those who can eat granulated sugar.
Plus baking without salt.

As we learn to eat healthier, we will make a difference in the
lives of those we truly love.

Illustrations by Caroline Martin
Self-Published by Caroline Martin@
Earlyharvest2012@gmail.com
Proofread by Missi Jo Morgan

Table of contents and recipe layout by Jeffrey Goettemoeller @
Prairie Oak Publishing 402-617-9118 or PrairieOakPub@gmail.com

1

Disclaimer
These recipes and health notes are not meant to replace the advice of a licensed
health practitioner. This recipe book is written for information and healthier eating
purposes only. It is not intended to provide all available information on the subject
matter covered.

While every effort has been made to insure the accuracy of this book, there may be
mistakes in content and typography. The author and publisher assume no
responsibility or liability with respect to any alleged or real damage caused, directly
or indirectly, by information contained in this book.
If you do not want bound by this disclaimer, you may return the book to the
publisher or store for a full refund.

Table of Contents

Acknowledgments

First and foremost, I acknowledge my Lord and Savior, Jesus Christ. He is the light that lights my path, and the unseen guide for my feet. There have been many knots and tangles putting this book together. Many times I have asked Him to inspire me when I felt like giving up, or didn't want to work on it at all.

I am truly blessed to have a dedicated husband. If it wasn't for him supporting me, and helping to proof read my book time and time again, and making sure I had the money to buy things I needed, I would not have been able to move forward with this book. Thank you so much my faithful husband. God truly made you my earthly hiding place. Words can never express the inner peace I have just knowing God and you will always be here for me.

I also would like to give great thanks to Missi Jo Morgan. I was truly blessed when I saw she threw herself into proofreading my book, and at the same time Missi also did her best to edit as well. Although it was her first time ever to attempt to edit or proofread anyones book, I feel she did an outstanding job for the first time. Missi jumped into it with feeling and care. I saw she truly cared, and wanted my book to be something I would be proud of. I'm so thankful and blessed that God used Missi to help me in my times of frustration. I look forward to hopefully working with her next year on my second edition. Thank you Missi, I'm deeply thankful and blessed by the work you did for me.

I also feel the need to express much appreciation to these companies: Enjoy Life semi-sweet chocolate Mini Chips, Madhava Naturally Sweet Organic Coconut Sugar, and Bragg Liquid Aminos. I appreciate that they allowed me to use their names, and to take photos of their products. These products are mainstays in my kitchen.

I also wish to express much appreciation to these two health food stores:
Natures Pickin's and Sunny Bridge. They were a great help to me over the past 3 ½ years.

Introduction

Growing up on a farm 98% of our food was from the land, grown naturally. We were strong and healthy children. We lived 12-15 miles from town and about 2/3 of a mile into the woods. Our nearest neighbor also lived about 2/3 of a mile away. I have no memories of going into town much, only to school–a two room school house about 3 miles away.

My father died when I was about eight years old. At that time, life became too real for a little farm girl. The good clean healthy life came to an end. I started eating foods I had never seen before. My mother was at a loss, but did the best she could. My memory of hundreds of canning jar lids sealing with a loud "pop pop" late into the night and the sweet smells of pepperoni sticks hanging from our basement floor beams had come to an end. I can still see jars and the wood burning cook stove that had served up these healthy memories. Homemade hotdogs, too sweet butter, and cottage cheese had vanished. As had that mother who had worked from sun up to sundown, and long into the night, making certain there was food for her brood. One night when I was 4 or so, I was up with her while she was canning apple sauce. She filled my heart with song, singing "Mama's Little Baby Loves Shortening Bread".

My mother was always coming up with great foods. God had blessed her with the skill to cook–no need for a recipe. As a spring continues to flow, that gift was passed down to me.

I love to feel good. I have so much to do in life, and if I don't take care of myself in a healthy way, I am no good to anyone. God says "train up a child in the way he should go and when he is old, he will not depart from it" (Prov 22:15).
This is so true. I turned away from eating healthy for a time...but I came back to it.

Let's try to feed our hearts, souls, minds, and bodies with food that will build us up...not break us down.

I do enjoy eating like everyone else, and like everyone else, I am tempted to eat things that are unhealthy for me just about every day. I find myself in a war between eating healthy or unhealthy.
This cook book will help you in your battle to eat healther.
Keep it on hand, use it as much as you can, and start to feel the pure benefits from eating healthier.

How to Use This Book

"Beyond Wheat" is a book for those of us who want more out of life. I want to feel good seven out of seven days. I strive to do so all the time, and enjoy good health along with my husband. The recipes in this book are easy to make. One way I make things easier is by preparing things ahead of time. One of the main stays I keep handy at all times is my "milled seed mix" (See page 10).

I believe if we learn to eat to be healthy, and not just eat because we can, we'll feel healthier.

Take your first steps to eating better...feeling stronger...and thinking clearer.

Health Benefits of Buckwheat

The three sided buckwheat groat has the shape of a beechnut, and shares the same rusty color when it's toasted.

Although it is called buckwheat, it is not wheat.

Buckwheat has been used for some 500 years or so, and has many medicinal benefits such as:

- Supports the large intestine, stomach, and spleen.
- Moves slowly through the gut, thus giving a "full" feeling.
- Stabilizes blood sugar irregularities, including diabetes.
- Contains D-chiro-inositol found to be deficient in type 2 diabetics.
- 100% naturally gluten free.
- Neutralizes toxic acidic wastes.
- Reduces cholesterol.
- Contains rutin, quercetin, and flavonoid glycosides.
- Helps some people with high blood pressure by dilating the blood vessels, thus reducing capillary permeability. This results in increased circulation in the veins, thus lowering blood pressure.
- Increases circulation to the hands and feet.
- Mitigates varicose veins, bruising, and damage from frostbite and radiation.
- Buckwheat is high in all eight essential amino acids, and it is higher than all other grains in lysine, making it a good protein source. Buckwheat also has up to 100% more calcium than other grains.

Reference: The New Whole Foods Encyclopedia.
 * These statements have not been evaluated by the FDA.
The information is not intended to diagnose, treat, cure, or prevent any disease.

Ingredients

This book's main ingredients are:

- buckwheat flour
- buckwheat toasted groats
- oat bran
- milled flax and milled chia seeds
- coconut sugar

It's important to remember you're not working with wheat. Buckwheat flour, oat bran, milled flax, and milled chia seeds swell when wet. They are stickier than wheat. They are also easier to clean up, making your work time shorter, and that's great.

A note to remember: When buying your coconut sugar, BE SURE TO BUY THE BEST BRAND! You may need to try more than one brand before you find the one you like, but it will be worth it. I use Madhava Organic Coconut Sugar in just about all of my recipes.

All Purpose Shaker Mix and Seed Mix

First make some chia and flax seed mix. You can buy whole seeds and mill them yourself or buy them already milled. Mill and mix together:

> 1 part chia seeds
> 1 part flax seeds

One part can be 1 cup or 1 pound–it's what works for you. When seeds are milled and mixed well, pour into freezer bags and store in the refrigerator or freezer until needed. For the All Purpose Shaker Mix, combine:

> ¾ cup milled seed mix
> 1 ½ cups oat bran

I put my All Purpose Shaker Mix in a parmesan cheese jar, and store it in the refrigerator. It is very important to keep your milled seeds in a very cool place or in your refrigerator because the milling makes them oily. It can cause them to become rancid if they aren't stored properly.

Helpful hint: It is much simpler to mix the seeds together for storage before you mill them. In the beginning, I had two containers lined up on my counter. This left me less room to work. That's when I was blessed with the idea to mix the seeds together, and store the mixture in bags in the refrigerator. It sure has been a blessing. I get done in half the time.

Make sure you always have this All Purpose Shaker Mix on hand. It's your help in time of need. Sometimes when I am out of, let's say, for example one of my hot cereal mixs; I need to get my husband off to work, and I only have about 40 minutes. I'll grab the rolled oats...pour some into a bowl, shake in some All Purpose Shaker Mix, throw some nuts in with it, and it's ready for the boiling water.

Toasted Buckwheat Groats

I always keep toasted buckwheat groats on hand. You can buy them toasted or toast your own. I preferred to toast them myself until I found a company that toasted them the way I like them. To toast buckwheat groats, pour some on a cookie sheet and, place in a 325° oven. Stir until golden brown...but do keep a close eye on them. When done, let cool on cookie sheet.

Then pour them into freezer bags, and store in a cool dark place or freezer or refrigerator. I keep a pint jar in my refrigerator so I can shake them into my recipes, on salads, or on top of hot cereals. I don't really like my groats cooked up in my cereal so I just shake some on top of my hot cereal.

Coconut Sugar

I use Madhava Organic Coconut Sugar in just about all my recipes. Keep in mind that coconut sugar has a little stronger taste to it than cane sugar, and much darker.

Those of you who can't use cane sugar will enjoy these sweet treats.

Important note: If you're not sure you can use coconut sugar in your diet, check with your health care practitioner.

Enjoy and eat to your health.

Chapter 1

Breakfast Is Served

Cereals

What better time to start eating healthy than at breakfast?! Having a cold cereal mix handy is a great way to save time and still eat healthy. These cold cereals are great for kids too–they don't come from a box, but from Mom's heart. You can't get any healthier than that!

Again, the sweet wisdom came from above. One day I wanted something cold for breakfast, not just my hot cereal mix's that I would sometimes eat cold. I just put a little this and a little that into a bowl and sat down to eat it. Guess what?! A new recipe was born.

Learn to make and keep these 3 great cereals on hand. Instead of reaching for that "box"from the store, you'll have your own, and that's a great feeling because you know it's a healthie cereal!

The Cereals with the Crunch

Continued on next page

Quick Start Peanut Raisin Cold Cereal

1/3 cup milled seed mix
1 ½ cups oat bran
¾ crushed salt free peanuts
¾ cup toasted buckwheat groats
¾ cup raisins
Sweeten to taste

Pour ½ cup cold cereal mix into bowl. Add 2/3 to ¾ cups milk. Top with some fruit. Makes: about 6 servings. Store remainder of cereal in refrigerator.

SMOOTHIE RECIPE

½ cup Peanut Raisin Cereal
2 ½ to 3 cups milk of your choice
½ apple
¼ cup plain yogurt
Sweeten to taste
Makes: about 4 ¼ cups.

To make Chocolate Peanut Raisin Smoothie
 Just add 2 tbsps cocoa powder.

Place all ingredients in a blender. Mix only until creamy.
Refrigerate and use within 2 days.

This is my 11 year old grandson enjoying one ofhis Grams Peanut Raisin Smoothies. He is one great baseball player. He always has the power within to play-play-play! It's very important for him to eat a very healthy diet. My smoothies are one great way for his growing body to get a healthy start. They will help to keep him playing for a long time!

Quick Start Walnut Chocolate Chip Cold Cereal

  1 ½ cups oat bran
  1/3 cup milled seed mix
  ½ cup crushed walnuts
  2/3 cup toasted buckwheat groats
  ½ cup semi-sweet Enjoy Life mini chocolate chips
Makes: about 6 servings.

Prepare same as for "Quick Start Peanut Raisin Cold Cereal" (see page 14)

SMOOTHIE RECIPE
  ½ cup Chocolate Chip Cereal
  2 ½ to 3 cups milk of your choice
  ½ apple
  1 ½ to 2 tbsps cocoa powder
  ¼ cup plain yogurt
  Sweeten to taste

To make Walnut Chocolate Chip Peanut Smoothie

Add ¼ cup of peanuts. Place all ingredients in a blender.
Mix only until creamy.

Makes: about 4 ¼ cups. Refrigerate and use within 2 days.

Quick Start Walnut Orange Cold Cereal

1 ½ cups oat bran
1/3 cup milled seed mix
½ cup crushed walnuts
2/3 cup toasted buckwheat groats
1 tsp cinnamon
½ tsp nutmeg
2 tsps dried granulated orange peel
 Makes: about 6 servings.

Prepare same as for "Quick Start Peanut Raisin Cold Cereal" (see page 14)

SMOOTHIE RECIPE
½ cup Orange Walnut Cereal
2 ½ to 3 cups milk of your choice
½ apple
¼ cup plain yogurt
Sweeten to taste

To make Chocolate Walnut Orange Smoothie

Just add 2 tbsps cocoa powder.
Place all ingredients in a blender. Mix only until creamy.
 Makes about: 4 ¼ cups. Refrigerate and use within 2 days.

Homemade Syrup for Health Bars and Granola

l cup maple syrup
l cup cane sugar
4 tbsps organic coconut oil

NOTE: Organic coconut oil has a real coconut taste. This will give your health bars or granola a great coconut flavor.

Place all ingredients into 1 quart sauce pan. Turn heat down low when syrup begins to boil, and let it cook for about 10 to 15 minutes. When syrup begins to boil, stir now and then with a spoon to be sure syrup doesn't stick. Begin to test syrup within 10 minutes. Test syrup by allowing a little to drip off the spoon. If the syrup slowly forms into a long thin thread, it is ready to be poured over the cereal mix.

If you like health bars or granola here are 3 great recipes from my Quick Start Cold Cereals and my Unforgettable Rolled Oats Hot Cereal recipes.

All photos are of my Unforgettable Rolled Oats Bars

 Continued on next page

Orange Walnut Crunch Bars

2 cups orange walnut crunch cold cereal mix (see page 16)
¼ cup crushed walnuts or almonds (or mix 2 tbsp each to = ¼ cup)
¼ cup dried berries or raisins (or mix 2 tbsp each to = 1/4 cup)
1 ¼ cups homemade syrup (see page 17)

In a large bowl, mix all dry ingredients well. Pour 1 ¼ cup of the hot syrup over the dry ingredients.
Place into microwave for 1 ½ minutes, remove, and mix well.

While ingredients are hot, pour mix onto a 2-foot piece of parchment paper.
Pull parchment paper up around the mix, and form a hard ball. Pull paper down from around ball, and use a rolling pin to roll out mix to about ¼ to 1/3 of an inch thick. Let cool for about 10 minutes.

Cut bars with pizza cutter or sharp knife into the size you want. To make granola you only need to pour the mix onto the parchment paper and form into little granola pieces the size you want.

These are great health bars. They fill you, and they are very satisfying to your taste buds. Makes: about 6 bars (1/3 x 1 ¼ x 4 inches). Refrigerate leftover syrup to make more health bars later.

Peanut Raisin Crunch Bars
Follow same steps as Orange crunch bars, but use 2 cups Quick Start Peanut RaisinCold Cereal Mix.(see page 14)
If you want, you can add ¼ cup of dried berries.

Unforgettable Rolled Oats Bars

3 cups Unforgettable Rolled Oats Hot Cereal mix (see page 19)
½ cup crushed walnuts
½ cup dried berries or raisins (or mix ¼ cup of each to = ½ cup)
1 ¾ cups homemade syrup (see page 17)

Follow same steps as Orange Crunch and Peanut Crunch bars, but use 1 ¾ cup homemade syrup in your Unforgettable Rolled Oats Bar mix (heat for 2 minutes). Makes: about 8 to10 bars (1/3 x 1 ¼ x 4 inch bars).

Unforgettable Rolled Oats Hot Cereal

3 cups rolled oats

2/3 cup coarse oat bran

½ cup milled seed mix

2/3 cup crushed walnuts

½ cup toasted buckwheat groats

2 tbsps dried granulated orange peel

Makes: about 4 ½ servings.

Combine ingredients to make the dry cereal mix.

Prepare to eat: Pour 3 cups of water in a pot and cover. Bring water to a boil, and add 1 ½ cups of the dry cereal mix. Stir with a spoon until well blended. Turn heat down to low, and cook without the lid for about 2-3 minutes. Stir only one more time before serving... or bring water to a boil, pour cereal in, turn heat off, stir, and cover. Let set for about 2-3 minutes–cereal is less mushy. Enjoy this healthy hot cereal with some fruit on top or a hand full of raisins or berries. Sweeten to taste.

My two great hot cereals are truly a dream come true for the mom who wants to feed her growing cubs a healthy hot breakfast. This cereal is loaded with health benefits that plain cereals can't offer. Have you ever been told that there is more than one way to eat Rolled Oats? Well this is it!

Someone told me when she first tried my Rolled Oats cereal, she said it was "unforgettable" thus the name was born. I believe you'll feel the same way.

Creamy Cocoats Hot Cereal

If you love and believe in the power of chocolate, this creamy cereal recipe will get you started in your day, the chocolate way!

> 1 cup coarse oat bran
> 4 tbsps milled seed mix
> 1/3 cup cocoa powder
> 1/3 cup toasted buckwheat groats
> Makes: about 3 ½ servings.

To make larger amounts:
> 6 cups coarse oat bran
> ¾ cup milled seed mix
> 2 cups cocoa powder
> 1 ¼ cups toasted buckwheat groats

To make about 3 ½ servings, pour 2 1/3 cups water or milk into a pot. With lid on, bring water to a boil.

NOTE: If using milk, it is best not to use a lid because it will boil over. When it begins to come to a boil, turn water down on low. Stir in ¾ cup cereal mix with a whisk until
well blended. Cook for an additional 2 to 4 minutes, stirring 2 to 3 more times before serving. The longer it sets, the creamier it gets.

Two Quick and Just Right Homemade Syrup
for
Buckwheat Pancakes and Waffles

Maple Syrup

For buckwheat pancakes and waffles
  2 cups Madhava Organic Coconut Sugar
  ½ cup water
  2 to 3 tsps maple extract*
*This will depend on your taste, and if you use real or
imitation maple extract.
This syrup is just as good without any extract.
Try it both ways.

Add all your ingredients in a medium sauce pan.
Bring mixture to a boil, and turn heat down to low.
Stir now and then as it cooks for about 2 minutes.
Serve warm. Makes: about 1 cup.

Sweet and Sour Cranberry Syrup

  12 oz bag of fresh cranberries
  1 ¼ cups water
  1 2/3 cups cane sugar or Madhava
  Organic Coconut Sugar

Add all your ingredients in a medium sauce
pan. Bring mixture to a boil, and turn heat
down to low. Stir now and then as it cooks for
about 5 minutes. When done, pour mixture
into your blender. Blend until creamy.
Pour back into the pot, bring to a boil stirring
so syrup doesn't burn, and cook on low for
about 3 more minutes. Serve warm.
Makes: about 3 ¼ cups.

A Must Try: This Sweet and Sour Cranberry Syrup is unbelievable on the Sunny
Walnut and Apple Pancakes or Waffles. I don't normally like sour foods, but I do
love a sweet and sour taste on the right foods. I must say this is one of the right
foods! I just fell in love all over again, no not with my husband. Yes, he can truly
be sweet and indeed sour, but my new love is the buckwheat Sunny Walnut
pancake or waffles with this sweet and sour syrup!

To make waffles size 6"-7"

There's no greater way to start your day than the buckwheat pancake way!

You won't believe their taste! These cakes are so filling and very satisfying. You and your family will want to eat them every day, and just maybe one later for a snack.
These buckwheat pancakes and waffles freeze well–I always keep a stack in a bag in my freezer.

For pancake recipes: see pages 23 - 24.

Use any of these pancake recipes for Buckwheat Waffles, but use only 4 cups of water. Let batter "rest" for about 12 minutes. If you like thinner waffles, add a little more water (about ¼ -1/3 cup).

Pour ½ cup of batter onto heated waffle maker (coated with a little oil for each waffle).
Lightly spread batter out to cover ¾ of waffle iron. Bake accordingly.
Makes: about10-12 Waffles.

Here I laid out three steps for making these Buckwheat Waffles.

22   Continued on next page

Deep Dark Chocolate Pancakes

2 cups buckwheat flour
¾ cup milled seed mix
1 ¾ cups cane sugar or Madhava Organic Coconut Sugar.
½ cup oat bran
2 tbsps + 1 ½ tsp baking powder
¾ cup cocoa powder
2 eggs
¼ cup cooking oil
4 ¼ cups water
   Makes: 18-24 small pancakes.

For pancakes:
In large bowl, mix all dry ingredients well. Make a
hole in the center of the mix. Add eggs, oil, and 4 ¼
cups of water. Mix well. Let batter rest for about
5 minutes. Batter will become thicker.
Always stir batter down before frying. If you like
thin cakes, add ¼ - ½ cup more water.
Do not make batter too thin. Right before pouring
batter, add a little oil to your skillet. Use a ¼ cup to
pour your batter.
These cakes are thick, so turn heat down to low.
Turn cakes over when they look a little dry around
the edges and a little bubbly on top.

These chocolate pancakes are great with peanut
butter. Make those little growing bodies a healthy
peanut butter snack. Take two of your Deep Dark
Chocolate Pancakes, spread some peanut butter over
one, and lay the other one on top. There you have
it… a healthy sandwich for any chocolate lover.

To prepare waffles: see page 22.

          Continued on next page

Sunny Orange Walnut Pancakes

2 cups buckwheat flour
¾ cup milled seed mix
1 ¼ cups cane sugar or coconut sugar
½ cup oat bran
2 tbsps plus 1 ½ tsp baking powder
3 tsps cinnamon
3 tbsps orange peel powder
½ cup crushed walnuts
2 eggs
¼ cup cooking oil
4 ¼ cups water

*Prepare all pancakes same as Deep Dark Chocolate Pancakes (see page 23).

Pumpkin Walnut Pancakes

3 cups buckwheat flour
¾ cup milled seed mix
1 ½ cups cane sugar or coconut sugar
1 cup oat bran
2 tbsps + 1 ½ tsp baking powder 2 tsps nutmeg
3 ½ tsps cinnamon
3 eggs
¼ cup cooking oil
4 ½ cups water
1 cup pumpkin
Add pumpkin to wet ingredients.

Sweet Potato Pancakes
2 cups buckwheat flour
¾ cup milled seed mix
1 ¼ cups cane sugar or coconut sugar
½ cup oat bran
2 tbsps + 1 ½ tsp baking powder   3 tsps cinnamon
3 tbsps orange peel powder
½ cup crushed walnuts
2/3 cup raisins
2 eggs
¼ cup cooking oil
4 ¼ cups water
1 cup pureed sweet potato (add last)

To prepare all Waffles: (see page 22)

Walnut Apple Pancakes

2 cups buckwheat flour
¾ cup milled seed mix
1 ¼ cups cane sugar or coconut sugar
½ cup oat bran
2 tbsps + 1½ tsp baking powder
3 tsps cinnamon
1 ½ tsps nutmeg
1 tbsp orange peel powder
½ cup crushed walnuts
1 medium size golden delicious apple (cut into 1/8 inch pieces)
2 eggs
¼ cup cooking oil
4 ¼ cups water

24

Buckwheat Corn Pones

2 ¼ cup buckwheat flour
2 cups oat bran
1 cup corn meal
1 ½ tsps sea salt
¾ cup cane sugar or Madhava Organic Coconut Sugar
2 tbsps + 1 ½ tsp baking powder
½ cup milled seed mix
3 eggs
¼ cooking oil
4 ½ cup water

(Prepare same as Deep Dark Chocolate Pancakes see page 23).
Do not make the batter too thin or the corn pones will be too
flat. If corn pones are too thick, add 1/4 - 1/2 cup more water.
Use ¼ cup to pour batter with for corn cakes.
If you want corn pones, use a tablespoon to drop batter into the
hot oil (drop slowly into hot oil to not burn yourself).

Note: When making corn pones they always taste and look
better when fried in a little more oil (just covering bottom of
skillet). Oil it the same way every time right before frying a
new batch.

Makes: about 2 ½ dozen small corn pones or 18-24 small corn
cakes (these make great corn muffins and corn bread).

Breakfast Muffins

No time to eat...running late...don't want to stop along the way and pick up something that's not healthy? Just reach for your pre-made "breakfast" muffin and a big glass of milk...now you're good to go! It's best to bake large muffins because one can be your entire breakfast when you don't have time to sit down to eat, or you just don't feel like cooking breakfast.

These are great for children, too... You can feel good about giving them a breakfast muffin. They are full of all the healthy ingredients their little bodies deserve, and certainly healthier than a pop tart! Add a glass of milk to these powerhouse muffins, and your breakfast is complete!
Bake about 12 or so and store them in your freezer.

You can take it a step further and top them with that healthy cream cheese icing. They will melt in your mouth. (see page: 65)

Here are 4 great breakfast muffins that you and your family will fall in love with:

Plain Breakfast Muffins
- 1 ½ cup oat bran
- 1 cup buckwheat flour
- ½ cup milled seed mix
- 2 tsps baking powder
- 2 tsps cinnamon
- 1 cup cane sugar or Madhava Organic Coconut Sugar
- 2 eggs
- ¼ cup cooking oil or softened butter
- 1 cup water
- ½ cup apple sauce

Makes: 6 large or 12 small muffins.

Mix dry ingredients in a large bowl. Make a hole in the center. Mix together eggs, oil, vanilla, applesauce, and water. Pour into the hole in the dry ingredients. Mix well.

Fill WELL GREASED muffin cups about 2/3 -3/4 full. Bake in a 325° oven for about 20-25 minutes. Test a muffin in the center of pan by inserting a toothpick in the center of the muffin. Muffins are done when the toothpick comes out clean. When done, remove from the oven, and let cool for about 3-5 minutes before removing from the pan.

Continued on next page

Walnut Raisin Muffins

Prepare as plain muffins except:
Fold in ¼ cup crushed walnuts and 1/3 cup raisins.

Walnut Raisin Carrot Muffins

Prepare as above except:
Fold in ¼ cup crushed walnuts, 1/3 cup raisins, and replace apple sauce with ¼ cup packed, finely shredded carrots.

Walnut Raisin Pumpkin Muffins

Prepare as above except:
Fold in ¼ cup crushed walnuts, 1/3 cup raisins, and replace apple sauce with ¼ cup pumpkin.

Chapter 2

Lunch Is On

Salad Shaker Mix

 1 cup toasted buckwheat groats
 2 cups milled seed mix
 4 cups coarse oat bran
 2 tbsps granulated orange peel
 2 tbsps granulated lemon peel
 3 tsps black pepper
 3 tbsps onion powder
 3 tbsps garlic powder
 1 tsp paprika
 1 tbsp sweet basil and Italian seasoning
 ¼ cup parsley flakes
 2 tbsps ground cumin
 2 ½ tbsps coarse sea salt
 3 cups parmesan cheese
Makes: about 10 cups.

Pour all ingredients into a large bowl. Mix well.

This Salad Shaker Mix is great to use on your salads. Place some in a parmesan cheese jar and refrigerate. Put remainder in freezer.

Rich Robust Salad Dressing Mix

2/3 cup each: sunflower seed oil, olive oil, and hemp seed oil. Add 1/3 cup Gluten free Liquid Aminos All-Purpose Seasoning from soy protein. If you like your salad dressing a little sweet, add Madhava Organic Coconut Sugar. Sweeten to taste. Place in pint jar. Shake well. Refrigerate.

This makes a great healthy salad dressing.

Unbelievable Soups

Seasoned with the Perfect Gluten free Soy Sauce Alternative:
Liquid Aminos All Purpose Seasoning from soy protein.

Soups are one of the ways to fill a healthy appetite. They are more than a three course meal. They are rich in flavor and very filling. Lentil soups, for example, are rich in fiber.

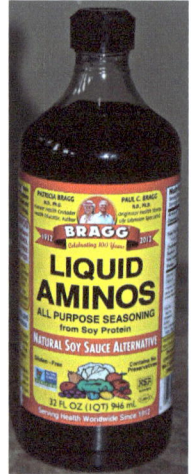

When making soups, use your "All Purpose Shaker Mix" and toasted buckwheat groats and add a little to the soups, thus giving them more fiber (see page 10-11).

Homemade soup is the best. When it starts to cook, and the rich smell fills the house, your taste buds start to kick in! I can be outside working in my yard when the smell of cooking soup reaches my nose, and I can't wait until it's time to eat! I especially love winter. The windows are closed; I come in from outside, and the smell raps around me. It pulls my spirit into a world of God's wonderful blessings.

The word "soup" goes back thousands of years. When Jesus had His last supper with his disciples, Jesus tells how He gave the "sop" unto Judas Iscariot before Judas went to betray Him (John 13:26). The word "soup" means "sop." Before spoons were invented people would take a crust of bread, and use it to ladle the liquid from the bowl. When the crust was no longer useful, it would be eaten as well. What a way to end a great meal!

Split Pea Chowder

1 lb. bag of mixed split peas, yellow and green hulled barley, and green and red lentils **
9 to 10 cups water
¼ cup olive oil or butter
¼ cup Gluten free Liquid Aminos All Purpose Seasoning from soy protein
½ cup each: chopped onions, celery, and carrots
¼ cup whole kernel corn

** You can find this split pea mix in health food stores and some grocery stores. To make your own, just mix 1/2 cup of each type of pea.

Makes: about 10 to 12 servings.

Clean and wash your split pea mix. Pour into crook pot. Add all the ingredients above.
For dry seasoning, use Lots "O" Bean Soup ingredients (see page 33).
Cook on high until well done.
I love this Split Pea Chowder. It has the same texture of real chowder. What a wholesome meal! You need nothing else but the corn muffins, corn pones, or corn bread (see page 25).

Grandmother's Onion Soup

      8 large onions (red or white)
      ½ cup butter or olive oil
      4 quarts water
      ¼ cup Gluten free Liquid Aminos All Purpose Seasoning from soy
      protein
      ½ cup toasted buckwheat groats
      ½ cup All Purpose Shaker mix
      1 ½ tsps black pepper
      3 tsps sea salt
Makes: about 14 servings.

Peel and cut onions in half from top to bottom. Slice onions. Place into 6 quart soup pot (cover). Sauté the onions in the butter until brown, stirring so they won't stick. Add water and other ingredients to browned onions. Bring soup to a boil, and then reduce heat to low. Let simmer, stirring soup 3 to 4 times. Cook for about one hour. Serve this creamy onion soup with wheat free crackers or wheat free croutons. Place shredded cheddar cheese on top of each bowl prior to serving.

Helpful hint: Make your soup and refrigerate it for about 2 days before serving. This makes your soup richer and full of flavor. It's like Grandmothers… they improve with age.

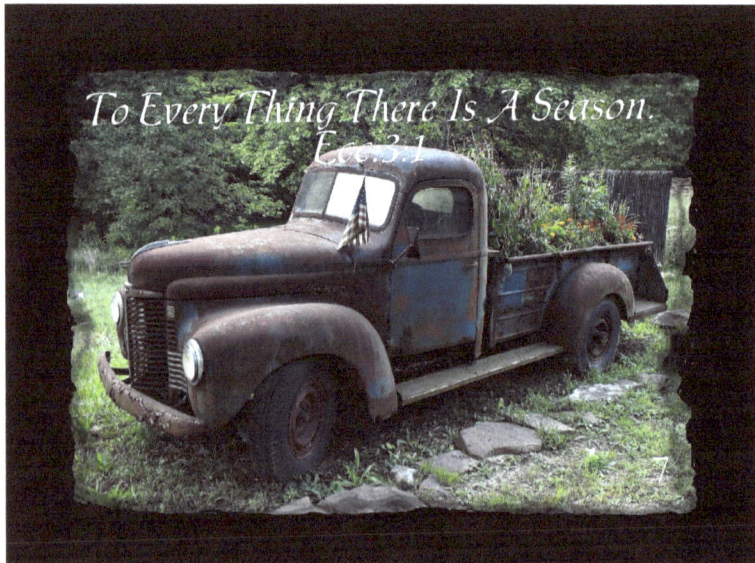

To Every Thing There Is A Season. Ecc.3.1

Lots "O" Beans Soup

1 lb. bag of mixed beans
9-10 cups of water (or more if you like it thinner)
2 tbsps Gluten free Liquid Aminos All Purpose Seasoning from soy protein
1 tbsp Worcestershire sauce
¼ cup butter or olive oil

Wash and clean beans. (To quick soak, pour boiling water over beans and let set until doubled in size).

Clean and rinse beans before cooking.

For dry seasoning:

2 tbsps each: black pepper, garlic powder, onion powder, and cumin
1 tbsp parsley flakes
1 tbsp sea salt
1 tbsp oat bran
3 tbsps milled seed mix
¼ cup toasted buckwheat groats

Makes: about 12 servings.

Place all ingredients (above) in crock pot. Turn on high. Cook until done.
When beans are cooked, remove about 3 cups of the bean broth and pour into a pot. Add ¼ cup each: chopped onions, celery and carrots. Sauté until done. When sautéed mix is done, pour back into the pot of beans. Stir well. Serve up with some fresh hot corn pones (recipe page 25).

Winter Chili

1 lb. bag of kidney beans (black, red, or mix black and red to = 1 lb.)
¼ cup butter or olive oil
1 cup chopped onion
1/3 cup chopped sweet red pepper
1/3 cup chopped green pepper
1 ½ cups chopped or crushed tomatoes
½ cup tomato paste
3 tbsps Gluten free Liquid Aminos All Purpose Seasoning from soy protein
8-10 cups water
2 cloves of garlic (leave whole, then crush in the chili when done).
1 ½ tbsps chili powder
1 tbsp sea salt
1 tsp oregano
Use "Lots "O" Bean Soup dry seasoning mix" (see page 33).

Clean and quick soak beans (see page 33).
When doubled in size, drain and pour into large soup pot.

Add all other ingredients. Cook on high until chili comes to a boil.
Then turn heat down to low, cover, and simmer until well done.

He Sendeth forth His Commandment
Upon Earth:
His Word Runneth Very Swiftly.
Psa:147:15

12

Topping for Your Winter Chili

Put ¼ cup butter into skillet along with 2 cups chopped onions, green and red sweet peppers, and ¼ cup hot peppers. Sauté for about 5 minutes. When done, add 1 cup whole kernel corn. Frozen corn is best, but make certain it has no water or ice in it. Stir into onion mix, place the lid on the skillet, turn off, and let set for about 3-5 minutes.

Crush 5 cups of corn chips in a large bag. Then, top each bowl of chili with ¼ cup crushed corn chips and the sautéed onion mix. After that, top each bowl of chili with ¼ cup shredded cheddar cheese.

Boy "O" boy… now bring on the snow and the fried corn pones. Serve it up with the sweet blessings of God, and you'll have a warm feeling inside and out.

Makes: about 7-9 servings.

Black Noodle Soup

2 large onions (sliced)
4 cups of cabbage (cut into about ½ inch cubes)
2 cups carrots (cut into ¼ inch pieces)
3 tbsps olive oil or butter
3 ½ quarts water
1 tbsp sea salt (more or less to taste)
3 tbsps All Purpose Shaker Mix
½ to ¾ cup Gluten free Liquid Aminos All Purpose Seasoning from soy protein
1 lb. buckwheat noodles made 1/8 to ¼ inch wide (see page 39- 40)

In a large soup pot, sauté all vegetables for about five minutes in the butter or oil. Then add the water, Liquid Aminos, salt, and the All Purpose Shaker Seasoning mix. Stir until well blended.

With the lid on the pot, bring soup to a boil, stirring 3-4 times. Turn heat on low and cook for about five minutes more, stirring now and then. Add the noodles to the soup. Cook for about 15-20 minutes longer until noodles are done.
Makes about: 9-10 servings.

What is the reason for calling the buckwheat noodles black? It's because buckwheat flour is milled with the hulls on. These hulls are dark brown, making the flour a little gray. So when baked or cooked in any form, the flour will be dark, almost gray/black.

Remember all the health benefits of eating buckwheat. You can fully enjoy this noodle soup because it is naturally wheat free, and it doesn't lay heavy on your stomach.

Heart Warming Vegetable Soup

1 cup carrots (cut into ¼ inch pieces)
½ cup dry chick peas
½ cup dry navy beans
Clean and quick-soak beans until doubled in size (see page 33).
2 cups crushed tomatoes
1 cup pizza or pasta sauce
2 cups frozen peas
2 large stalks of celery with leaves (cut into ¼ inch pieces)
1 large onion (cut into ¼ inch pieces)
1 medium sized potato (cut into ¼ inch pieces)
1 cup frozen corn
1 cup cabbage (cut into ¼ inch pieces)
¼ cup toasted buckwheat groats
3 tbsps All Purpose Shaker Mix
¼ cup barley
3 tsps sea salt (to taste)
2 tsps black pepper (to taste)
1 tbsp garlic powder, cumin, and paprika
¼ cup fresh or dried parsley flakes
2 tbsps Gluten free Liquid Aminos All Purpose Seasoning from soy protein
3 quarts water
¼ cup olive oil of your choice
2 tbsps butter

Makes: about 9-10 servings.

Put all ingredients into a large soup pot. Bring soup to a boil, then turn heat down on low, and cover with the lid. Cook until well done (about 1 and ½ hours). Serve with wheat-free crackers and cubed cheese of your choice.

This heartwarming soup is wonderful on a cold winter day. Winter time is a blessing from our God because it makes us slow our pace and enjoy each other more. It calms our minds and relaxes our bodies. It is "ONE BIG TIME OUT". So enjoy this wonderful gift, and the time will pass before you know it! Soup is not just for winter. You need to enjoy it year round. Remember all the health benefits of soup.

Enjoy your soup with Corn Dogs and homemade French fries.

Chapter 3

Dinner A Waits

Buckwheat Noodles

1 ½ cups buckwheat flour
½ cup fine oat bran
2 tbsps milled seed mix
1 tsp sea salt
½ tsp black pepper
1/8 - ¼ cup water
3 eggs
1 tbsp Gluten free Liquid Aminos All Purpose Seasoning from soy protein
1 tsp olive oil

In large mixing bowl, combine all dry ingredients. Make a hole in the center of the dry mix. Mix eggs, oil, Liquid Aminos, and 1/8 of cup water together. Then pour it into the hole. Mix well. Dough will be a little dry (dough must be dry so it can be kneaded). If dough is too dry, add water a small amount at a time until you can make it into a ball. Dough will be hard to work with. There will be some dry spots, and some flour in the bottom of the bowl. Now pour dough onto a buckwheat floured surface. Knead it with the heel of your hand. Keep turning, folding, and pushing it down with the heel of your hand until the dough has no more dry flour in it. The flour you put onto the surface will be worked into the dough. Keep working the dough with the flour.

Now make a ball that you can hold in your hand, but keep the surface floured so you can roll your dough onto it. Roll the dough out until it's about 1/16 inch thick. Make your dough as thin as you can. With a pastry wheel, pizza cutter, or sharp knife, cut dough into long strips or for lasagna cut into 2 inch wide strips.
Makes: about 1 - 1 ½ lbs. noodles.

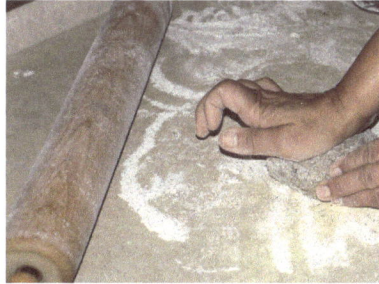

Continued on next page

To cook noodles:

*Pour 4 cups of water in a 4 quart sauce
pan. Add: 3 tbsps Liquid Aminos,
2 tsps garlic powder with parsley flakes.*

When water and seasoning begains to
boil, place about ½ of the noodles into it.
Let cook about 5 minutes.
When done remove noodles.

Add 4 more cups of water too sauce pan and the *ingredients above.*
When water and seasoning begains to boil add rest of noodles.

When noodles are done, you can cut them into small pieaces or leave them long.

Serve them as you like. You can add them to soups or cook them with chicken to
make chicken and noodles.

With a little imagination, these noodles will go a long way. Don't look at the color
of your noodles–just remember the health benefits from eating buckwheat.

Buckwheat Dumplings

1 1/3 cups buckwheat flour
½ cup oat bran
2 tbsps milled seed mix
1 tsp baking powder
1 tsp sea salt
½ tsp black pepper
3 tbsps wheat free Liquid Aminos All Purpose Seasoning from soy protein
½ cup water, chicken, or beef stock broth (for firmer dumplings, use 1/3 cup water, chicken, or beef stock broth).
3 eggs

Makes: about 2 lbs.

In large bowl, combine all dry ingredients. Make a hole in the center of the dry mix. Add eggs, wheat free Liquid Aminos, and water. Mix well. Let batter rest for about 15 minutes. The dumplings will be better if you allow the mixture to rest.

To cook dumplings:
Take two small spoons (larger spoons if you want dumplings bigger) and drop them by the spoonful into your boiling soup or stock broth. Keep the spoon at the level of the hot liquid to keep from splashing yourself. Continue adding dumplings until they cover the top, and you can't see any liquid. Cover with a lid and turn the heat down on low, letting the dumplings simmer until done. If you want the dumplings to be nice and round, you can use an ice cream scoop.

These Dumplings freeze very well. Here I have them laid out on a cookie sheet so you can see them. Freeze them for about 3 hours. Then place them in a freezer bag. Return dumplings to the freezer, and use as needed.

Make the family a big pot of chicken and dumplings, and enjoy the healthy taste and richness of buckwheat.

Helpful hint: if you dip your spoon into the hot liquid the dumplings will come off easier.

Fried Cabbage and Noodles

1 large head of cabbage (cut in half)
2 tsps garlic powder with parsley flakes
1 ½ tsps black pepper
¼ cup Gluten free Liquid Aminos All Purpose Seasoning from soy protein
1 large onion
½ cup cooking oil
¼ cup water

To fry the cabbage:
Cut the cabbage head into halves, then cut the halves into ½ inch long pieces,
and then cut the long pieces in half. Cut onion in half, cut into ¼ inch slices then
cut them in half. Place all ingredients in large skillet with cabbage and onions.
Turn down on low.

Let fry until cabbage starts to brown, turning cabbage over to keep from sticking.
When cabbage is ¾ done, add 1 cup water and about 2 cups buckwheat noodles
 (See page 39 - 40). You can cut them in little pieces or leave them whole.
Makes: about 6 – 8 servings.

Serve up your cabbage and noodles with some buckwheat corn dogs (see page 43).
What more do you need?

Buckwheat Corn Dog and Hush Puppy Batter

1 cup buckwheat flour
½ cup corn meal
¼ cup oat bran
2 tbsps milled seed mix
¼ tsp black pepper
½ cup onions (finely chopped)
½ tsp sea salt
2 tsps baking powder
1 tsp garlic powder
2 eggs
2 tbsps olive oil
1 tbsp Gluten free Liquid Aminos All Purpose Seasoning from soy protein
1 ¼ cups water

Makes: about 8 corn dogs.

In large bowl, combine all dry ingredients. Make a hole in center of dry mix. Add water, eggs, olive oil, and Liquid Aminos. Mix well. Let rest for about 5 minutes.

Heat 4-5 cups of cooking oil in a 4-6 quart sauce pan. Lay dogs on a towel, and dry them well before dipping them into the batter. You can cut your hot dogs in half, or leave them whole.
Makes: about 8 servings.

When the hot dogs are dry, stir the batter well before frying. Then with a fork, dip one at a time into the batter, completely covering the dog. Drop slowly into the hot oil to prevent splashing and burning yourself. *Repeat the same process until you have 2 or 3 dogs in the hot oil. Turn them frequently so they brown evenly.
Have a paper towel lined plate ready for the finished "dogs."

Helpful hint: You can test the oil to make sure it is hot enough by dropping a little of the batter into it. If it rises to the top immediately, the oil is ready.

Continued on next page

Hush Puppys

You can keep unused batter to make hush puppies. Just add about ¼ cup more corn meal. Add a little at a time, and mix until well blended. You don't want the batter too thick… just thick enough to stay on the spoon. Drop slowly into the oil to prevent splashing and burning yourself. Repeat the same process until you have dropped enough hush puppies into the hot oil. Turn them frequently so they brown evenly.

Serve up your hush puppies with homemade coleslaw, fish, and french fries. Or keep your hush puppies for a quick healthy snack.

Try dipping them in mustard and ketchup. It brings out their flavor even more.

*My husband and I really like these corn dogs. It's a good feeling to know that they're healthier for us than wheat.

Buckwheat Deep Fried Fish Batter

Use buckwheat corn dog batter (see page 43), but add 1 tbsp more of Gluten free Liquid Aminos, 1 ½ tsps more of garlic powder, and 1 ½ tsps more of sea salt. Be sure to chop onions very fine. Prepare same as corn dogs.

To deep fry fish:

Make sure fish is dry before dipping it into the batter. You can cut it the size you want. Use only thick pieces of fish, and use tongs to dip fish into batter–not a fork. Let some batter drip off the fish before dropping it into the hot oil. Drop the fish slowly into the hot oil to prevent splashing and burning yourself. Turn them frequently so they brown evenly.

Makes: about 1-1 ½ pounds.

* Make hush puppies with unused batter (see page 44).

Buckwheat Breading for Meats and Vegetables

And Meat Additive

3 cups milled seed mix
4 ½ cups oat bran
2 cups buckwheat flour
1/3 cup parsley flakes
¼ cup onion powder
¼ cup garlic powder
4 ½ tsps black pepper
¼ cup cumin
1 tbsp sea salt
3 tbsps paprika

Makes: about 10 cups.

In large bowl, combine all dry ingredients. This breading is great on all meats, fish, and vegetables. *Also use in all ground meats* Dip your meat or vegetables in some water or Liquid Aminos, and then roll it in the breading. Bake or fry your meats, fish, or vegetables. You will love the way this breading makes your meats, fish, or vegetables taste. They are so moist and full of flavor.

The breading on the baked fish is milled buckwheat groats without the hulls, making it lighter in color.

Breaded Baked Fish

Breaded Fried Turkey

Meat Loaf

When using my Breading Mix (see page 46) in these mouthwatering recipes, there's no need for eggs or bread crumbs.

> ½ cup breading mix (see page 46)
> 2 lbs. of ground meat of your choice. This breading is great for ground turkey–makes it moist and holds it together while giving it a mouthwatering taste.
> 1/3 cup parmesan and Romano cheese
> ¾ cup homemade pasta sauce
> 2 tbsps Gluten free Liquid Aminos All Purpose seasoning from soy protein

Mix all ingredients together in large bowl. Then make one big loaf or two small loaves.
Place into baking dish and bake at 300° until done.
Makes: one big loaf or two small loaves.

To make meat balls

Prepare same as meat loaf (see page 47), but make it into meat balls. Fry meat balls in a small amount of oil, turning them so they will brown evenly. Fry only until they are about two thirds done. Then add meat balls to your pasta sauce, and cook about a ½ hour to 45 minutes with heat down low. Makes: about 15 medium-size meat balls.

Country Fried Steak

Prepare same as meat loaf(see page 47), but make ½ to 2/3 inch thick patties about
4 inches long and 2 ½ to 3 inches wide. Then pour some breading mix onto a plate,
and roll your steak in it about 3 times to be sure the steak is well coated. Place into
a preheated skillet with a little cooking oil. Set heat on medium to low. Fry steaks
on both sides until golden brown and well done.
 Makes: 6-8 steaks.

These country fried steaks freeze well. Here I have layed them out to freeze. Just
place them in your freezer for about 2 hours, then place them in a freezer bag for
later.

Chapter 4

Sweets On The Side

**One Bite
    For You,
        and
The Rest
    For Me!**

Chocolate Chip Pie Crust

¾ cup cane sugar or Madhava Organic Coconut Sugar
¼ cup fine oat bran
2 cups buckwheat flour
6 tbsps milled seed mix
¾ cup coconut oil or shortening (room temperature)
½ cup water (room temperature)
2/3 cup finely crushed walnuts (add last)
1/3 cup Enjoy Life Mini Chocolate Chips (add last) Check
at health food store for sugar free chocolate chips.

Makes: 2 cream pie crusts.

In large mixing bowl combine all dry
ingredients.

Cut in coconut oil or shortening with
mixer on low speed until mix resembles
coarse crumbs. Sprinkle water over
mixture. Toss with large spoon until
ingredients are moistened.

Add chocolate chips and walnuts. Mix
only until well blended.

Make sure mixture is wet enough to
shape into 2 firm balls. Lay a large
piece of plastic wrap on the counter,
and sprinkle with buckwheat flour.

Continued on next page

Roll dough out onto floured plastic wrap about 1/8 inch thick. Lay pie plate upside down over rolled-out dough.

With your left hand, hold two corners of the plastic wrap. Slide your right hand under rolled-out pie dough. Flip pie plate and pie dough over at the same time.

Work dough down in, around the sides, and around the top of the pie plate.

Helpful hint: Don't be upset if your dough breaks in some places. Just take that piece and press it back into the spot it fell from, or if it cracks just pull it back together. You'll never know you patched it. I do it all the time. Your first pie crust will be a little hard to do, but the more you make the better you'll get. And believe me you'll want to make more of this pie!!

Shape the edge of pie dough with fingers or fork. Prick bottom and sides of dough with
fork, then place on cookie sheet.

Bake in a 325°oven until crust is firm to the touch. You may need to lay a piece of parchment paper or foil over pie crust if they're baking too fast. Remove pie crust from oven, and cool on wire rack.

Fruit Pie Crust and Apple Dumplings

¾ cup cane sugar or Madhava Organic Coconut Sugar
¼ cup fine oat bran
2 cups buckwheat flour
6 tbsps milled seed mix
¾ cup coconut oil or shortening (room temperature)
2 tsps cinnamon (fruit pies only)
½ cup water (room temperature)

Makes: Dough for 1 Double-Crust Fruit Pie or dough for 4 to 6 apple dumplings.

To make crust for 1 fruit pie:

Prepare as for cream pie crust (see page 51). Go through the same steps in rolling out the dough. Roll out bottom crust the same as for cream pie, except brush some milk or heavy cream around the edge before laying top crust on it. This helps the bottom and top crust to seal together.

Roll dough out on plastic wrap for top crust , place one hand under rolled-out dough, and flip dough over fruit filling. Shape pie crust edge, cut slits in top, and brush top with heavy cream before baking. Bake in a 325° oven for about 45 minutes, or when fruit is fully cooked. Cover pie with parchment paper or foil if it begins to brown too fast.

Fresh out of the oven

You must bake this pie for your family. Believe me, it's not that hard to make, and you'll be surprised at how good it will taste!

Apple Dumplings

Use fruit pie crust for your Apple Dumplings (see page 53). Prepare crust as for cream pie crust (see page 51- 52). Go through the same steps in rolling out the dough, except cut rolled out dough into 6 to 9 inch squares. Peel and core 4 to 6 apples or pears, and place onto each dough square.

Mix together:

 ¼ cup cane sugar or Madhava Organic Coconut Sugar.

 ¼ tsp cinnamon

 ¼ tsp nutmeg

Sprinkle over fruit. Brush edges of dough with milk or heavy cream.
With plastic wrap under dough square, fold corners to center on top of fruit. Take both hands and press dough around fruit. Remove plastic wrap. Place apple dumplings upside down in a 7 ½ x 12 x 2 ½ inch baking dish.

 Syrup mix for dumplings:

 ¾ cup cane sugar or Madhava Organic Coconut Sugar.

 ½ tsp cinnamon

 ½ tsp nutmeg

 1 ¾ to 2 cups of water

Mix all ingredients in a sauce pan. Bring syrup mixture to a boil. Reduce heat. Simmer 2-4 minutes. Turn heat off, add 3 tbsps butter, and mix well. Pour syrup over dumplings. Bake in a 325° oven for 30-40 minutes or until fruit is tender, and the crust is brown. If they are browning too quickly, cover with parchment paper or foil. When done, remove from oven and cool on wire rack.

Poppa's Cream Cheese Chocolate Chip Chunk Pie

While pie crust is baking (pie crust recipe on page 51 - 52), make your pie filling.

> 4 cups milk - of your choice
> 2 tbsps butter
> ½ cup cocoa powder
> 1 ¾ cup cane sugar or Madhava Organic Coconut Sugar
> 7 tbsp cornstarch
> 4 egg yolks
> ¼ cup milk – for the corn starch
> 1 tsp vanilla – add last.
> Two 8-oz packages of cream cheese (room temperature for about 1 hour)
> Filling for 2 pies

Pour milk into a 2-quart sauce pan. Add butter and sugar. Stir with whisk, then add cocoa powder (be sure to use a top brand). Turn heat down low. Let cocoa set on top of milk for about 5 to 8 minutes, or until cocoa begins to dissolve. Then stir with wire whisk until cocoa is completely dissolved.

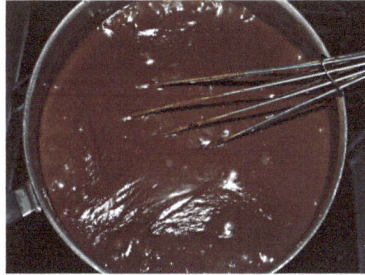

While your milk mixture is getting hot, mix together your egg yolks and the ¼ cup of milk. Add the egg mixture to the corn starch, and stir with a wire whisk until rich and creamy. Make sure there aren't any lumps. Then turn heat up and bring milk mixture to a slow boil. Slowly add the egg mixture into the boiling milk, stirring as you pour. Turn heat back down to low, and continue stirring so your pudding does not burn. Cook for about 5 to 7 minutes longer.

Turn heat off, stir in the vanilla, place lid on pot, and set pudding aside.
Place cream cheese into a large mixing bowl. Turn mixer on low until cream cheese is broken up, then turn up to medium.
Scraping the sides of the bowl, mix cream cheese until smooth and creamy. Turn mixer back down on low. Pour in pudding mix. Once blended, turn mixer back up to medium. Continue to mix until creamy, and then pour pudding into your baked pie shells.
Lay a piece of plastic wrap on top of pies, and set in refrigerator for about 8 hours before serving.

Continued on next page

Helpful hint: Laying plastic wrap over your pies will keep them from drying out. Remove pies from refrigerator, remove plastic wrap, and top your pies with homemade whip topping. Makes: two 9-inch pies.

Enjoy this rich creamy pie over a cup of hot green tea or a nice fresh cup of coffee, and with some good uplifting conversation with family and friends or the lonely person next door.

You can freeze your pies. Here I have laid some out to freeze. Freeze for about 2 hours, and then place in freezer bags. Let pie set out for about 20 minutes or microwave 30 seconds before eating.

Fudgy Buckwheat Fudge Cake

Preheat Oven to 325°
  2 cups buckwheat flour
  1 ¼ cups dark cocoa
  ¼ cup milled seed mix
  ¾ cup fine oat bran
  2 tbsp + 1½ tsp. baking powder
  2 ¼ cups cane sugar or Madhava Organic Coconut Sugar
  2 eggs
  ½ cup cooking oil
  2 ¾ cups water

In a large bowl, combine all dry ingredients. Make hole in center of mixture. Pour in eggs, oil, and water. Mix until well blended. Let batter rest for 1 minute befor pouring it into pans.

Pour immediately into 2 WELL GREASED 9 ½ x 1 ½ inch round cake pans.

Bake in a 325°oven for 25 to 30 minutes or until toothpick inserted near center of cake comes out clean and pulls away from sides of pan.

 Makes: two 9 ½ inch x 1 ½ inch round cakes.

Remove cakes from oven. Cool upside down on racks lined with parchment paper or saran wrap for 3-5 minutes then remove pans - tapping bottom and sides for easier removal. Place cakes in freezer for about 1 hour.

Continued on next page

Chocolate Glaze for Fudge Cake

2 cups Enjoy Life Mini Chocolate Chips
¾ cup butter
*There is now a sugar free brand of
chocolate chips which maybe found in
your local health food store.

To make chocolate glaze:
Place chips and butter into a 1 quart sauce
pan. Turn heat down on low. As chips begin
to melt, stir, and keep stirring until glaze
becomes smooth and creamy. Remove cakes
from freezer and place one cake on a cake
plate. Pour ½ cup of the glaze over top of
the cake. With icing spatula, spread glaze
over top of cake. Allow a little of the
glaze to flow over the sides.

Remove ½ cup more of the glaze, and set
aside. Place the other cake on top of the
first cake.

Pour remaining glaze over the top of the cake,
spreading and allowing glaze to flow over the
sides. Work glaze around the sides until the
whole cake is covered. Pour the remaining ½
cup of glaze around the edge of the top cake.
Allow the glaze to flow down the cake in long
droplets. Sprinkle with coconut flakes if you
like.

This cake just melts in your mouth. Knowing
the health benefits of this cake lets you enjoy it
even more. So take some next door and share
it and sit down to a nice hot cup of coffee or
a cup of green tea, and share the blessings.

Brownies and Cookies
From Fudgy Buckwheat Fudge Cake Mix (See page 57)

To make brownies:
Just add 1 ¼ cup crushed walnuts to cake mix. Pour into well-greased 11 x 16 x 1 inch cake pan. Bake the same as Fudge Cake. Bake for 15 to 25 minutes or when toothpick inserted in center of brownies come out clean, and the sides pull away from pan. When done, cool on a rack. Glaze (see page 58) or enjoy just the way they are.

Is he dreaming or what? My 6 year old grandson truly knows how to enjoy chocolate, especially topped with homemade whipped topping!

To Make Walnut Chocolate chip Cookies: Use only 2 ¼ cups of water in your cake mix. Blend well, then fold in 1 ¼ cup crushed walnuts and 1 cup of large chocolate chips. Use 2 tablespoons to drop the cookies onto the cookie sheet. Scoop up dough with 1 tablespoon, then scrape the rounded cookie dough off with the other spoon about 2 inches apart onto a cookie sheet that is lightly greased or lined with parchment paper.

Bake in a 325°oven for 6 to 10 minutes, or test one cookie by pressing down lightly on center. If a little firm to the touch, remove from the oven. Let the cookies cool about 1or 2 minutes before removing from cookie sheets. **Helpful hint:** If using parchment paper, just pull paper off onto counter with cookies on it. That makes it easy and fast. You're free to keep on baking those healthy mouthwatering chocolate chip cookies!
Makes: about 3 to 5 dozen.

Buckwheat Quick Apple Crisp

Preheat oven to 400°

      ¼ cup fine oat bran

      2 cups buckwheat flour

      ½ cup crushed walnuts

      ½ tsp cinnamon

      ¾ cup cane sugar or Madhava Organic Coconut Sugar.

      6 tbsps milled seed mix

      ¾ cup shortening or coconut oil (room temperature)

      ¼ to ½ cup cold water

      About 8 to 10 Golden Delicious apples

Makes: about 12 servings.

In a mixing bowl, blend all dry
ingredients. Cut in ¾ cup shortening or
coconut oil. Sprinkle cold water over
mixture. Gently toss with fork while
adding water a little at a time until dough
forms into small and large crumbs. Place
in refrigerator until needed.

To make sauté mix:

Peel and core apples, and cut them into ¼ to 1/3 inch thick pieces. Place the apples
into a deep skillet, and sauté in 3 tbsps of butter. Bring to a boil. Then reduce heat
to low for about 3 minutes with lid on. Turn heat off. Add 1 ½ tsps cinnamon, ¾
cup sugar, and ½ cup water. Stir until well blended.

Continued on next page

While the apples are sautéing, place a 13 x 9 x 2 ½ inch glass baking dish on the top rack in a 400° oven. When apples are done, pull hot dish out of oven, and place on pot holders.

Put 2 to 3 tbsps butter in the hot dish, coating all sides.

Pour hot apples into the hot dish. Sprinkle crust crumbs over apples, and bake in a 400°oven on top rack until the apples start to boil. Then turn the heat down to 325°, and bake 8-10 minutes or until the topping is hard to the touch and browned. Remove from oven. Cool on a rack.

Helpful hint: If you like your crust topping thinner, just set some aside and bake it on a cookie sheet. You can use it for a crunchy topping over cereal, fruits, ice cream, yogurt, or bag it up to use for a midday snack. Kids will love these little crunchy treats, too. Serve warm with homemade cool whip.

Goodness right out of the oven.

Apple Raisin Walnut Upside down Cake

Preheat oven to 325°

2/3 cup cane sugar or Madhava Organic Coconut Sugar

1 ½ tbsps baking powder

½ cup fine oat bran

2 tbsps milled seed mix

¼ cup buckwheat flour

1/3 cup butter or coconut oil (melted not hot)

2/3 cup water

2 eggs

Bottom:

1 extra-large golden delicious apple

2 heaping tbsps raisins

3 tbsps butter

1/3 cup cane sugar or Madhava Organic Coconut Sugar

¼ cup water

¼ cup crushed walnuts

Core and peel apple. Cut apple in round slices like a pineapple, then cut in ¼ or 1/3 inch slices. Place into skillet with butter. Turn heat down on low and cover with lid. Sauté apple slices for about 4 minutes. Remove them with slotted spoon and set aside.

To make bottom:

Pour raisins, sugar, walnuts, and water into the same skillet. Stir well and let cook on low for about 2 minutes with lid on. When done, pour sautéed raisins, walnuts, and sugar in a 9 ½ x 1 ½ round cake pan. Arrange apples on top of sautéed mix.

Continued on next page

To make cake mix:

Mix all dry ingredients well in a large bowl. Make a hole in the center of the dry mix. Add eggs, melted butter or coconut oil, and water. Mix well. Do not let batter set.

Pour over arranged sautéed apple mixture.
Pouring around pan slowly so as not to move sautéed mixture.
Work your way to the center of the pan, making sure to cover the bottom of the pan.

Bake in a 325° oven for 25-30 minutes or until a toothpick inserted into the cake near the center comes out clean. Lay a plate over the cake; turn upside down on plate, holding plate tightly. Let the cake set in pan about 3 or 4 minutes. Tap bottom and sides of pan, then remove pan.

You can also use peaches, pears, pineapples, or berries for this moist, healthy cake.

Serve up warm. Watch your family make it disappear. You're not only feeding their bodies, you're also feeding the souls that gather around your table. So take time to sit down and share the blessings that God has seasoned your lives with. Servings: about 8.

Pumpkin Raisin Spice Cake Bar
Or
Carrot Raisin Cake or Cup Cakes

        1 cup buckwheat flour
        ¼ cup milled seed mix
        ½ cup oat bran
        2/3 cup raisins
        1 tbsp + 2 tsps pumpkin pie spice
        1 tbsp baking powder

Mix dry ingredients well. Set aside.
----
        2 large eggs (if small use 3)
        ¾ cup pumpkin
        1 ½ cups cane sugar or Madhava Organic Coconut Sugar
        1/3 cup cooking oil or butter (melted not hot)

Place the bottom group of ingredients in large mixing bowl, and beat on low until creamy. Add the already mixed dry ingredients to creamed mixture, blend well. Add ¾ cup water, and mix until creamy. Pour into well-greased 10 ½ x 15 ½ inch cake pan, and spread batter evenly in pan. Bake in a 350° oven 20-25 minutes or until toothpick inserted into cake near center comes out clean.

 Cool cake in pan on rack. When cake is cool, cut to 3 inches wide x 10 ½ inches long. You should get 5 pieces of cake, but you'll only be using 4 of them to make your cake bars. You may want to make one of your cake bars 3 high. Or cut the fifth piece of cake in small pieces and serve with a little love, and a cup of tea!

Helpful hint: Lay the 4 pieces of cake on a cake pan and place in the freezer for about 30 to 45 minutes. By doing this, it will make icing the cake much easier. The top of the cake will not peel off when spreading the icing on it.

Continued on next page

To make icing:

    1 8 oz package cream cheese (room temperature)
    ¼ cup butter of your choice (room temperature)
    ¾ cup cane sugar or Madhava Organic Coconut Sugar

Place all ingredients into **warn** mixing bowl. Beat on medium until very creamy. This makes only enough icing for 2 cake bars.

Icing your cake bars:
Remove cakes from freezer. Place one piece of cake on a cake plate. Icing the top only, then place another piece of cake on top of it, icing only the top of that one. Repeat with your other two pieces.
Helpful hint: There is no need to cut and stack your cakes into bars. You can leave it whole in the cake pan and ice it. You can also cut the cake in half, icing bottom and top, making a two-layer cake.

You may also want to make your children some cupcakes for a snack with this cake mix. If you don't have children, make them for your sweetie to take for a snack before lunch, and just maybe your sweetie won't reach for that candy bar!

To make carrot raisin cake:

Replace the pumpkin with finely shredded carrots.

To make cupcakes:

Just mix same as for cake mix. Mix and bake in muffin pan, and fill cups ¾ full. Bake same as cake. Makes: 6 large or 12 small cupcakes.

  These healthy cup cakes are stacked high with a whole lot of goodness.

Pumpkin Raisin Cookies

Preheat oven to 325°

     1 ½ cups cane sugar or Madhava Organic Coconut Sugar
     ½ cup fine oat bran
     2 ½ cups buckwheat flour
     ¼ cup milled seed mix
     3 tsps pumpkin pie spice
     1 ¼ tsps baking soda
     2 eggs
     1 ½ cups pumpkin
     1 ¼ cups raisins
     1 ½ cups butter or coconut oil (melted not hot)

In a large bowl, mix all dry ingredients well. Make hole in center of dry mix. Add butter or coconut oil, eggs, pumpkin, and raisins. Mix until well blended.

Use 2 tablespoons to drop the cookies onto the cookie sheet. Scoop up dough with 1 tablespoon, then scrape the rounded cookie dough off with the other spoon about 2 inches apart onto a cookie sheet that is lightly greased or lined with parchment paper. Makes: about 3 to 4 dozen.

Helpful hint: Did you know that you could reuse your parchment paper over again? You can! About 5 or 6 times, if you don't burn it, maybe even more. This saves time and money.

Continued on next page

Take a spoon and press top of cookie dough down just a little. Bake in a 325°oven for 8 to15 minutes. Test one cookie by pressing down lightly on center. When it's a little firm to the touch, remove from oven. Let the cookies cool about 1or 2 minutes before removing from the cookie sheets.

Helpful hint: If using parchment paper, just pull paper off onto counter with cookies on it. That makes it fast, easy, and you're free to keep on baking!

These cookies are very moist. Do not leave them out. When cool, store in the refrigerator or freezer.

Buckwheat Ginger Snaps

2 ¼ cups buckwheat flour
½ cup fine oat bran
¾ cup packed cane sugar or Madhava Organic Coconut Sugar
¼ cup milled seed mix
1 tsp baking soda
3 tsps ginger
2 tsps cinnamon
½ tsp cloves
2 eggs
¼ cup molasses, honey or home made syrup
½ cup melted butter and ½ cup cooking oil

Helpful hint: You can make your own syrup with ¼ cup boiling water and 1 cup coconut sugar. Stir well until sugar dissolves. Boil about 2 minutes. Set aside until cool. This home made syrup makes my cookies have a richer flavor. Keep leftover syrup to put on one of your mouthwatering Sunny Orange Walnut pancakes.

In a large mixing bowl, beat together on medium, eggs, homemade syrup or molasses or honey, butter, and cooking oil. Beat until creamy. In a medium size bowl, mix together all dry ingredients. Pour dry ingredients into egg mixture a little at a time until well blended.

To make cookies:
Use your fingers to pinch off about 1/8 to ¼ inch of the cookie dough.
Form dough into a ball, and lay on the cookie sheet lined with parchment paper (about 2 inches apart).

Continued on next page

Press dough down with your fingers to about ¼ to 1/3 of an inch thick.

Bake in a 325°oven for 8-12 minutes. Test one cookie by pressing down lightly on the center. If a little firm to the touch, remove from oven. Let the cookies cool about 1or 2 minutes before removing from cookie sheets.

Helpful hint: If using parchment paper, just pull paper off onto counter with cookies on it. That makes it fast, easy, and you're free to keep on baking those healthy snaps!

For dipping:
Let cookies bake a little longer until firm in center.
Makes: about 3 to 4 dozen.

Walnut Chocolate Chip Cookies

2 ½ cups buckwheat flour
¼ cup milled seed mix
½ cup fine oat bran
¾ tsp baking soda
1½ cups large chocolate chips (add last)
1 cup crushed walnuts
1½ cups cane sugar or Madhava Organic Coconut Sugar.
¾ cup butter
¾ cup melted coconut oil (not hot)
3 eggs

* You can now buy sugar-free chocolate chips at some health foods.

Pour walnuts, sugar, butter, oil, and eggs in a large mixing bowl. Beat on medium until well blended.

Mix all dry ingredients together in medium

size bowl, with chips, until well blended. Then add a little at a time to egg mixture. Beat on low only until well blended.

To make cookies:
Use 2 tablespoons to drop the cookies onto the cookie sheet. Scoop up dough with 1 tablespoon. Then scrape the rounded cookie dough off with the other spoon. Drop about 2 inches apart onto an ungreased cookie sheet or onto a parchment paper lined cookie sheet.

Bake in a 325° oven for about 8-10 minutes. Test one cookie by pressing down lightly on center. If a little firm to the touch, remove from oven.
Let cookies cool 2-3 minutes before removing from cookie sheet.

Helpful hint: If using parchment paper, just pull paper off onto counter with cookies on it. That makes it fast, easy, and you're free to keep on baking!

Cool and refrigerate. Freeze if not eaten. Makes: about 3 to 4 dozen.

My Top Secret Buckwheat Oatmeal Cookies

½ tsp baking soda
3 cups rolled oats
1 cup fine oat bran
1/3 cup milled seed mix
1½ cups buckwheat flour
3 tbsps freshly grated orange peel
2 tsp cinnamon
1¼ tsp nutmeg
¼ tsp cloves
¾ tsp ginger
1½ cups cane sugar or Madhava Organic Coconut Sugar
½ cup crushed walnuts (add last)
½ cup coconut flakes (add last)
1 cup raisins (add last)
3 eggs
1 cup butter or coconut oil (softened)
½ cup olive oil

Beat butter, olive oil, sugar, and eggs in a large bowl on low until well blended. Mix walnuts, raisins, and coconut flakes in a separate bowl. Set aside. Then in another large bowl mix dry ingredients together. Add dry ingredients to egg mixture little at a time (only until well blended). Now add your raisins, coconut flakes, and walnuts (mix only until blended).

To make cookies:
Use 2 tablespoons to drop the cookie dough onto the cookie sheet. Scoop up dough with 1 tablespoon, then scrape the rounded cookie dough off with the other spoon about 2 inches apart onto a greased or parchment paper lined cookie sheet.
Bake in a 325° oven for about 8-10 minutes. Test one cookie by pressing down lightly on center. If a little firm to the touch, remove from oven. Let cookies cool 2-3 minutes before removing from cookie sheet.

Helpful hint: If using parchment paper, just pull paper off onto counter with cookies on it that makes it fast, easy, and you're free to keep on baking!
Makes: 3 to 4 dozen cookies.

Cool and store in refrigerate or freeze. For dipping, let cookies bake a little longer until firm in center.

Continued on next page

This is my Top Secret Oatmeal Cookie recipe from when I baked them with wheat. When I started baking with buckwheat I just converted them over to my new ingredients, and made a change here and there. I feel they taste just as great. Their flavor gives my taste buds something to remember. I always want to go back for more. I hope you and your family will keep going back for more, and build some healthy members around your dinner table!

I believe:

All life flow comes from our Heavenly Father. The more we feed upon His words and try to always walk in His ways He'll give us health to our souls, peace of mind, joy to our hearts, and strength to press on, when it seems life has lost its sweetness.

From birth unto death our soul hungers for the sweet fulfilling goodness of the Heavenly Father. To know our Creator is to know fullness of unspeakable joy.

Our hunger can only be satisfied when we sit down to the table our Heavenly Father has prepared for us. (His word is our daily bread.)Galatians 6:8 Therein lies our strength and daily nourishment. Our souls become full and thus we are truly satisfied with unspeakable joy.© Luke 11: 2-4

Shop Uniontown's
Only

Get all your Health Needs for your Mind, Soul, and Body.

Right Here at Your Natures Pickin's.

464 Connellsville St Uniontown .Pa 15401

724-438-4211

SUNNY BRIDGE
Natural Foods & Café

tempt
your
taste-buds

Cafe & Gluten-Free Bakery

Cross the Bridge to
a Healthier Lifestyle

Groceries,
Supplements,
& Body Care

130 Gallery Dr., McMurray | 724.942.5800
SunnyBridgeNaturalFoods.com

www.ingramcontent.com/pod-product-compliance
Lightning Source LLC
Chambersburg PA
CBHW041425090426
42741CB00002B/32